HARCOURT

BRACE

JOVANOVICH

San Diego

New York

London

Photographs by
RICHARD BROWN
Essays by
REEVE LINDBERGH
WITH AN INTRODUCTION BY
NOEL PERRIN

THE VIEW FROM THE KING-DOM

A New England Album

FOR ELIZABETH AND SUSANNAH

Requests for permission to make copies of any
part of the work should be mailed to:
Permissions, Harcourt Brace Jovanovich, Publishers,
Orlando, Florida 32887.

"The Snow Man" copyright 1923 and renewed 1951 by Wallace
Stevens. Reprinted from *The Collected Poems of Wallace Stevens*, by
permission of Alfred A. Knopf, Inc.
The following essays by Reeve Lindbergh originally appeared
in these publications: "Leaves," *Vermont Life*, Autumn 1983; "The
Poultry Wars," *Country Journal*, December 1981; "The Fat of the
Fallow," *Horticulture*, June 1980; "December," as "Welcome to
December," in *National Wildlife Magazine*, December/January
1979; "November," *Country Journal*, 1977.

Library of Congress Cataloging-in-Publication Data
Brown, Richard, 1945–
The view from the kingdom.
1. New England—Description and travel—1981–   —
Views. 2. New England—Description and travel—
1981–   . I. Lindbergh, Reeve. II. Title.
F5.B876   1987   974'.043   87-223
ISBN 0-15-193637-4

Production supervision by Warren Wallerstein
Designed by Joy Chu

Printed in Japan
First edition   A B C D E

Contents

Introduction

VERY FEW of the fifty states in this country contain a kingdom. I'm aware of only two: Florida and Vermont. And Florida's is a few acres of outstandingly synthetic amusement park—that portion of Walt Disney World known to tourists as the Magic Kingdom and to Florida officials as one small chunk of the Reedy Creek Improvement District. (Some improvement.)

Vermont's kingdom is quite another matter. The Northeast Kingdom covers two thousand square miles and includes three counties. Especially in Essex County, the northernmost and easternmost of the three, you will find land wilder and more beautiful than most people have any notion exists in the eastern United States. The whole upper two-thirds of Essex County is a blank area on the map, and even the bottom third is improved only by scattered farms and by a handful of small towns. Take Guildhall, the county seat. It has a courthouse and a very beautiful town hall, built in 1795. It also has 202 inhabitants. I'm talking about everybody who lives in the whole thirty square miles of farm and forest that comprise the town (which anywhere outside New England would be called a township), not the much smaller number that lives in the actual village. A town like Averill has a population of about fifteen. That's low enough to please even Thoreau, who felt the proper population density of the United States would be one person per square mile.

Obviously the Northeast Kingdom is not a literal monarchy, like Belgium or Norway. But neither is it the invention of some chamber of commerce or tourist commission. The name was bestowed, or at least given currency, by the late Senator George Aiken, the most distinguished politician Vermont has produced in this century. (Yes, I'm aware there was a president named Coolidge.) That was back at the very beginning of Aiken's thirty-year career in the Senate and soon after he had ceased to be governor.

Furthermore, since *monarchy* means simply "rule by one person," there really was a time when a monarch possessed the principal territory of the Northeast Kingdom. His name was David Page. You can read about him in the second-earliest book ever written about Vermont, John Graham's *Descriptive Sketch of the Present State of Vermont*, published in 1797. "I well remember the person who settled in this quarter of the Country," Colonel Graham wrote, "and whose family was for many years the only one in it." He goes on to tell briefly about the further settling of the region, and then he concludes, "The emigrants who followed Mr. *Page* into the County of *Essex*, gave him the title of Governor, by which name he was known and acknowledged till his death."

The book you are about to read describes life in the Northeast Kingdom in the 1980s, some dozen years after a fresh wave of immigration. It's a good thing that one of the two authors is a brilliant photographer, almost certainly the best in the state, because pictures are needed. Colonel Graham, not a man to lack for words—he was one of the smoothest-tongued lawyers Vermont has ever had—simply gave up when it came to representing the landscape of the kingdom. After saying "the most romantic imagination can scarcely conceive anything more commanding," he tries for a paragraph to paint a verbal picture—"Towns rising above Towns in gradual succession," etc.—and then lamely concludes, "An adequate description cannot possibly be conveyed." Perhaps not. But Richard Brown's photographs do pretty well.

That's just the scenery. There are also the people of the kingdom—the most remote and Vermonty of all Vermonters. The whole state has a reputation for stubbornness, and the northeast corner is perhaps the most stubborn of all. Always has been. There was another early settler, in the county next to Page's, named William Barton. He was a revolutionary war hero, a fighting colonel. He was also, like practically all early settlers with either money or political influence, a mighty speculator in land. At least as the story is told, he got into trouble over titles and deeds, and rather than yield an inch, he spent fourteen years in the Danville jail. Stayed there until 1825, when the Marquis de Lafayette happened by during his famous American tour and promptly bailed the colonel out.

The whole state also has a reputation for egalitarianism and in particular for being a place where women farmed as freely as men, or ran businesses, or in more recent times got elected governor. Or welcomed visiting dignitaries, for that matter. During Lafayette's whole thirteen-month tour of America, just twice did a woman introduce him to the crowd. One of the two times was in Montpelier, Vermont.

Again, the state's wildest corner tended to have the freest women of all. There's a little town in the kingdom called Irasburg—named for Ira Allen, who with his brother Ethan had much to do with the founding of Vermont. Ira, who had plenty of land grants and not much else, gave Irasburg to his wife Jerusha as a wedding present. When he died broke, she calmly moved there with her son and started a sawmill. Which didn't keep her, as Graham says of the women of the kingdom, from being delighted "to form parties, and dance upon the green swerd, to instrumental, and sometimes to vocal music."

Reeve Lindbergh, as able and independent as any Jerusha Allen, and a much better writer, evokes present-day life in the kingdom as finely as Richard

Brown captures the landscape. I am struck in her essays with how much the recent immigrants to the kingdom have in common with the early settlers. There is the same combination of gaiety and of delight in hard work in a hard land. My one quarrel with Reeve Lindbergh is that she seems to me to lack a full appreciation of the pleasures of woodcutting—and a full understanding of why her husband spurns those miserable canvas wood-carriers and insists on bringing logs in by the armload, as all right-thinking people do. But to pursue that thought might be to get into ineradicable differences between how men and women perceive the dividing line between indoor and outdoor behavior.

The important thing is that in Reeve Lindbergh the Northeast Kingdom has found a worthy chronicler, and in Richard Brown a photographer who is her match. Between them they succeed in giving the account that Colonel Graham tried to, and failed.

NOEL PERRIN
Thetford Center, Vermont

A · U · T · U · M · N

LEAVES

Every autumn I tell myself I won't write one more word about leaves. After all, don't the leaves themselves say best whatever it is we stubborn and struggling country writers keep trying to say about them over and over? Isn't that heart-piercing annual performance really a statement in itself, fundamentally untranslatable into other terms?

Unfortunately, yes. The trouble with writers, though, is that for us reality has to be verbal, not simply visual. We are by nature unhappy about anything we haven't been able to "capture" like some exotic butterfly and pin securely to paper with our own carefully chosen words. We may pose as sensitive, passive souls, mere absorbers and transmitters of experience, but don't be fooled: we are ruthless hunters and stalkers, preying upon everything in sight. We want to surround the whole world, cast nets of language over it, and make it our prize. This is both the delight and the curse of our profession, an occupational ambivalence we share with visual artists like my photographer-husband. He, too, finds it hard to leave beauty alone or even to enjoy it very much when unaccompanied by the tools of his trade. (I will tell you in confidence that I am married to a man who once swore at a sunset—a spectacular one—because he didn't happen to have his camera with him.)

If writers and photographers are among the chief offenders in this respect, however, we are not alone. I think there are many people who cannot appreciate a natural phenomenon unless they have recorded it in some fashion. (Item: one sunset, preserved forever by camera, diaries, and paints and pencils.) But does the recording process really enrich us, or is it that we think we have transformed a volatile, temporal pleasure into something more substantial and worthwhile: a document suitable for framing, to be filed away eventually in the archives of our lives—wherever those may be?

What on earth is the matter with us all? Why can't we just look, the way children do, and be content? Sometimes I wonder if it isn't again the old human instinct for dominion that gets in our way as adults. A writer's control of language can lead her to the happy self-deception that she has controlled life itself, bent it to her will and turned it like a tamed river into channels of her own choosing. For the photographer, an arrested image may symbolize the actual stopping of the clock, that timelessness pursued by artists for centuries. And for all of us mortals, of course, there is the perpetually tantalizing illusion of immortality.

Anyone who has spent time in Vermont during peak foliage season will see the irony in this dominion-and-immortality theme at once, however. For a Vermont autumn is not subject to our control in any way. That is exactly what draws us to it. There is a wildness in nature now, a quality of light and color that goes beyond our understanding of things pretty or picturesque or even beautiful, into another realm altogether. And here lies the second irony, which is death. The truth is that we like these leaves because they are dying, so that wherever immortality is to be found, it is not here. We would not have the same response to the season if it were.

It is because the leaves are dying that we love their lively colors, recognizing these as a kind of crazy courage. We love, too, that last flare of light before winter comes, just as we love the tiny fireflies that cannot possibly illuminate the vast hot nights of August, or small children with flashlights and scary masks at Halloween—all the bright, brave things that go whistling off into the dark and lift our spirits almost painfully as they go.

And perhaps that is all we are trying to express when we write about the leaves, photograph the leaves, sketch or paint them, year after year. Perhaps we are not trying to arrest or even control the season, but simply pay tribute to it, take our hats off as it goes by, and remember the manner of its passing.

COLLECTING

Autumn is for collecting things. Everybody knows this, from the children who gather bright-colored leaves, caterpillars, milkweed pods, and other "Signs of Fall" for classrooms all over the state, to avid adults combing the back pastures, eagle-eyed and bramble-fingered, gleaning the last of the summer berries. In spring, with our new lambs and our seed catalogs, we are driven willy-nilly toward rebirth and renewal, but in autumn, with our slaughtered chickens and knitting books, we tend to be taken over by a rake-it-in-and-horde-it mentality that hovers right on the cutting edge of greed.

In general, the collectors in our area are serious about what they are doing because they have to be. They are the woodsmen who need to bring in several months' supply of potential warmth within a few short weeks, and gardeners who for years or even decades have counted on the preservation of homegrown vegetables to ease the pressure on family incomes. However, there are also plenty of more frivolous collectors: the pickers of wild asters and everlasting for autumn bouquets; the end-of-season antiquers who fill their station wagons with souvenirs of all shapes and sizes; and, of course, those friendly pilgrims who travel over the roads of Vermont each October, enjoying the foliage as well as the church suppers, craft fairs, and other community events that abound at this time of year.

As collectors, we are distinguished by our idiosyncracies. One of my neighbors has a fondness for butternuts, another for the sweet taste of apples picked just after the first frost. Some of the mothers in our village eagerly await the church bazaar every fall to stock up on extra-thick mittens and hats for their children. They know these particular hand-knit goods were produced with all the loving expertise and accumulated winter wisdom of a generation of Vermont grandmothers.

Some of us, weary of our own collections, are inexplicably attracted to those of other people. A family living along the road between the village and the dump takes shrewd advantage of this susceptibility, planning their autumn yard sale for a crisply beautiful Saturday, the one day of the week when our dump is open. Other families, traveling past this house with the hope of getting rid of their own unwanted items, find themselves tempted by the siren song of somebody else's old jigsaw puzzles, wobbly standing lamps, and used Halloween costumes.

Among collectors, there are many dauntingly well-organized traditionalists, people who line up their pickle jars in the cupboard in alphabetical order and arrange their ripening tomatoes along the windowsills in graduated sizes. But in my experience there are some wacky and unfathomable nontraditionalists, too, who collect things you would never have thought of, in quantities that boggle the mind. A neighbor went down through a trapdoor in his shed not long ago, intending to inspect the sills, and found his way blocked by thirteen one hundred–pound sacks of chicken manure. They had been stored there by his wife, an efficient and practical native Vermonter, who knew how valuable they would be when it came time to fertilize the garden next spring.

In my own household, there is a disturbing amount of inefficiency and impracticality clouding the whole collecting enterprise. I'm not sure why; maybe we just haven't quite got the hang of it. Oh, we bring in the firewood and the green tomatoes the way everybody else does, but somehow our tomatoes don't seem to lend themselves to graduated sizing—in fact, what with the strangeness of their sizes and shapes, I fear they are underachievers and won't graduate at all—while our other harvests are apt to be either unsatisfactory or downright bizarre.

Take skunks. Like the earwigs that find their way into every corner of my house each autumn, skunks, all uninvited, add themselves to our collection at this time of year. I am told that they are attracted to woodpiles and garages in autumn because they wish to spend the winter cuddling up as close as possible to us humans and to our garbage. This is a flattering but uncomfortable thought, as you never know where an approaching skunk will be at any given time or what might be on his mind as he makes his approach. An unexpected encounter can be startling at the very least. We have lost chickens to skunks more than once, the dog has compromised her dignity many times, and we have, I think, forfeited permanently the annual visit of a group of ladies who pass out religious tracts in our neighborhood, because the last time they came, a skunk had visited us only moments before. I liked the ladies but can understand their reluctance to spread our particular message.

To complicate matters even more, all the time we are collecting earwigs and skunks without meaning to, everything that we should be harvesting has "gone by," a country phrase I have heard applied impartially to produce and to people ("He used to be a good doctor, but now he's kind of gone by"), and one that always gives me the lost, lonesome feeling of having missed the last train home. Whenever I hear it, I am haunted by one specific and guilty nightmare: a parade of overripe vegetables from my own garden marches past me on its way to ruin. Reproachfully, they go by: cucumbers, corn, squash of all kinds, everything but the intransigent tomatoes I mentioned earlier, which in their green stubbornness not only don't "go by," but also don't even come close.

A kind of perverse, season-defying anarchy sets in around our place at harvesttime. The animals and the children feel it just as much as I do. If I send my daughter out to the barn to collect eggs, she is just as likely to come back with a handful of feathers instead. The reason? The feathers were pretty and easily accessible, being scattered all over the chicken room floor, whereas the eggs were nowhere to be seen.

"There may be some under the Bad Hen, but I was scared to look," the child further confesses. I nod understanding. The Bad Hen is a broody, sullen Rhode Island Red who has taken a stand—or rather, an extended sit—in one of the nesting boxes in our chicken room. She refuses to move, and like some snakes, she must be approached very fast and from just the right angle. Other- wise she will strike, and strike effectively.

I know that, in theory, the Bad Hen is protecting her eggs from fumbling fingers. I know also, though, that right now there are few if any eggs under her to protect. The days are getting shorter and the hen is getting older, and with such a combination of discouragements, productivity always dwindles. I sus- pect, therefore, that the Bad Hen is merely feeling defensive, like some of the rest of us, about how little she is accumulating at this busy, bustling moment in the rural year.

"It's not my fault!" she says with each vicious jab of her bad-tempered beak. I always try to give her a brief, reassuring pat as I remove my empty hand from the nest. I know exactly how she feels.

NOVEMBER

Almost everyone who wants to visit us in the country comes in August. A fair number return for weekends in September and October, when autumn is at its peak, but by November our many guests have dwindled to a scant and rather special few. The people who are with us now have usually arrived alone. Surprisingly often, they are single, widowed, childless, divorced—human beings pared to essentials, like the season, and drawn to it for personal reasons. Rather than rushing off to auctions or sweating out six sets on a local tennis court or baking bread for us in a country-kitchen rush of enthusiasm, as other visitors have done at other times of the year, they are more apt to move through the November landscape in a spirit of respectful observation. These are the bird-watchers, road-walkers, tree-sketchers, wall-sitters at the edges of stubbled fields. Aware, but not afraid, of the hunters in the woods and the bleakness of the landscape. They are in tune with what one visitor in her seventies called the "ambiguity of the season," a mood of mingled apprehension and relief that colors our days. Most importantly, they do not need to be entertained.

We welcome the November people for just this reason, because for us, as for anyone else who lives in the country, it is a busy month. The tension of preparing the house and barn in time for the long winter ahead is heightened every day by the change in the atmosphere. Each morning an increased tingling in the nostrils registers another step toward the deadline after which all preparations will be too late—the serious, accumulative snowstorms of December.

Before then the foundations must be banked and the doors and windows sealed, as much to keep out the cold as the mice, voles, and flying squirrels that turn up in force at this time of year. Wood must be cut and stored in the cellar for fireplace and stove; the winter's supply of hay and grain must be made available for daily feeding to the motley group of cows, horses, sheep, and goats that fended for themselves so nicely all summer.

Suddenly, after a season of laissez-faire animal husbandry, nothing can be taken for granted. We have let the chickens, ducks, and geese run wild in the barnyard for months; now we hope to find them before the fox does. Otherwise we will wake up one morning and discover that the goose is gone—or worse, partly gone.

Still, with the ambiguity that our friend suggests, the season holds out one promise along with several threats. At the end of all this life-sustaining activity, this hectic race for preparedness, there will be a time of surcease, of letting go, as we sink into the temporary gentling death of winter. And after all, despite its length and sometime harshness, winter is not intrinsically an ominous time of year. It is an essential part of the cycle, a resting time for the earth and many of its creatures and, at least in the country, for a good number of the human population as well. The most time-consuming agricultural season has passed. Haying and harvesting are over, while the vegetable garden has been put to bed under mulch and manure by the conscientious and has been abandoned by the merely harassed.

In November, even the air and the landscape around us show signs of a philosophical letdown. The quality of light is different. There is less of it, but it is also subtler and more diffuse. When it touches the leafless branches of the hardwoods across the valley there is a starkness in the look of individual trees against the skyline, but this is the only time of year when one notices, through a whole group of bare branches on a hillside, the enduring contours of the hills themselves, the real shape of the land.

I remember late one autumn flying over many miles of state forest in a small airplane and observing for the first time that the countryside had a shape, and how soft—almost furry—the rolling wooded terrain below me appeared. It looked to me as if the thousands of bare branches collectively constituted some benevolent, hairy covering for the animal that is the earth.

There is a kind of comfort in the very bleakness of the landscape at this time of year, some quality of release and repose that I am ready for, even if I know I will repudiate every ounce of it vehemently by the time that other in-between season—March/April—comes around again. But there is a difference between the sloping pastures of November, still covered with dry grasses that move in living swells of red and gold and brown when the wind blows, and the dead, dessicated look of late March, when the land has just shrugged off the snow cover and all vegetation lies flattened and exhausted. March reveals the matted strands of brown straw where the grass should be; moldy black leaves along the roadsides; crumpled and wan hayfields that seem barely able to breathe, convalescent after winter. In spring, rain is the healer, but for November the agent of change is the event for which we have all been waiting—the first real snow.

It is surprisingly beautiful, surprisingly gentle, and one is apt to greet it the way children do, with joy and wonder, forgetting for a moment that it marks the beginning of the hard times we have prepared for all season, that it is often the most dangerous snowstorm of the year, causing more accidents than any other. We are never as fully prepared as we think. Many of us need a little time to effect the transition from summer to winter driving habits; we forget snow tires and antifreeze in the midst of our other preparations. We have to reequip the tractor, exchanging the mowing attachments of summer for the snowplow and the long chain that will be needed to pull friends and relatives and their out-of-state vehicles out of the ditch at the bottom of our hill.

All the same they continue to come, the loyal few. The closest among them will be with us for Thanksgiving, my personal favorite holiday of the year. On that day we will all give thanks for whatever manner of harvest has come to each of us during the past year, and perhaps feel thankful also for the season itself, which has allowed us this one contemplative lull and the presence of friends who appreciate it as fully as we do. With the hay in the barn and the wood in the cellar, it is not a comfortless thing, on a darkening afternoon at the end of the last month before winter, to sit with close friends around the Thanksgiving table and face, through a well-caulked window, that ambiguous November horizon.

W · I · N · T · E · R

WINTER MIND

One must have a mind of winter
To regard the frost and the boughs
Of the pine-trees crusted with snow;

And have been cold a long time
To behold the junipers shagged with ice,
The spruces rough in the distant glitter

Of the January sun; and not to think
Of any misery in the sound of the wind,
In the sound of a few leaves,

Which is the sound of the land
Full of the same wind
That is blowing in the same bare place

For the listener, who listens in the snow,
And, nothing himself, beholds
Nothing that is not there and the nothing that is.

—*Wallace Stevens, "The Snow Man"*

I have loved the poetry of Wallace Stevens for many years, but I am still not sure that I understand what he meant by "a mind of winter." I am watching the first flakes of the first snow outside my window, and winter is certainly on my mind. But "a mind of winter"? It is an unusual image, and especially intriguing to those of us living in northern Vermont, where winter occupies our territory and preoccupies our thoughts for almost half of every year. Perhaps if I lived here long enough I would acquire the right kind of mind to accommodate our longest season, but I have a hunch that these things do not come to us automatically just because we move through years or times of year. Even in Vermont, human beings have a tendency to resist improvement.

Would "a mind of winter" really be an improvement, though? What would it be like? Would it be a cold mind? A clean mind? A mind capable of forgetting all the sins and disorders of previous seasons, the way the snow smooths over and forgives the patches of leaves that were not raked away from the old stone wall, the undivided crowds of iris and daffodils at the edge of the lawn, the toy tractor left near the brush pile we never got around to burning?

Acceptance would have to play an important part in a mind truly attuned to winter, I suppose, but the very idea of "acceptance" at this season raises a storm of questions for me. Should I cease to put up such a fight? Welcome the drifts and the driving conditions with a humbler spirit? Stop worrying over weather reports, complaining about February, and comparing subzero readings on our thermometers with those of our neighbors?

Few of us who live this far north can afford to be so passive, especially at this time of year. Just to stay alive, we must take up arms (and axes and snowshovels and whatever else we need) against the extremes of weather that confront and confound us. Regardless of our seasonal philosophy, we absolutely have to do our shoveling of snow and our stoking of fires. We have to keep our hats pulled low and our fingers dry. The season gives us no other choices.

I think we may have to do our comparing and complaining as well, if only to make our presence known to one another during a time of increased isolation. There is something infinite about the silence outdoors now, some immensity in the gap between snow and stars, and it feels good to us to fill that space with noise. Cheerily we insist upon our own existence as we chatter and socialize our way through the winter months. "Are you still here? Well, good! So am I!" we signal into the stillness, fending off infinity with our own warm breath.

Infinity is not a cozy concept at any time of year, and although Stevens' man of snow may be perfectly comfortable with it, most of the rest of us are not—especially in winter. Now more than ever, we concentrate upon the finite. We know exactly how many logs have to go into the wood stove at night to keep the sleeping family warm in mid-January, and how many bales of hay and scoops of grain must be fed to the barn animals to maintain their health, and how many pairs of socks will protect the feet of the small child walking to the bus stop. These numbers make up the necessary equations of survival where we live. In a family, they also serve as a subtle measure of our love.

At a time when it is important to us to keep things simple, we strive with the simplest of mathematics for equilibrium. Complexity is only a nuisance when the temperature is below freezing. Abstract notions are apt to get in the way if there is real work to be done, and the snow man's poetic "nothings" may seem irrelevant if one's feet are cold. Still, as I stand by my window and watch the snow deepen and soften the landscape, I wonder if all our years here haven't taught us, like the snow man, to take the winter on its own terms. We have become equal to it and are therefore part of it, as it is part of us. The snow touching the earth now touches me, too, with its quietness, with my own quietness, and with a sense of welcome. I invite the first storm of the season gently and willingly into my Vermont winter mind.

5 5

DECEMBER

In our part of the world, winter is a serious business, and by December it has forced all of us to change our habits. For the human population, at least that part of it represented by our small family, the process is fairly simple. We get up earlier; dress ourselves and our children more warmly; carry blankets, snowshovels, buckets of sand, and booster cables in the back of the car; drink hot soup at lunchtime; and try our best to go about our business in spite of the season.

For the animals in our environment, it is more complicated. The deer who grazed freely through our pastures and the old orchard in early November are nowhere to be seen. The first deep snowfall confines them to their wintering yards in swamp or forest; their survival from now on will depend mainly on the weather. Other creatures, lucky or not according to your perspective, will have to depend on us. Flocks of sparrows, chickadees, nuthatches, woodpeckers, and grosbeaks who abandoned our dooryard for the summer now congregate at the feeders, hoping we have not forgotten them. In the barn, the cows and sheep, the goats and ducks, the geese and chickens all make anxious bids for our attention, each in its own manner.

It amuses me that the two horses who board with us change their tune so dramatically at this time every year. Not long ago, my husband and I spent a frustrating and wet day wallowing through muddy fields to catch them and bring them into the barnyard. I lost my boot and my husband lost his temper. But now when I walk out of the house, the flighty pony whinnies at the sight of me, while the ancient workhorse, two thousand pounds of stolid self-interest, lumbers up to the fence and gazes adoringly into my eyes.

"Cupboard love" is what my mother calls this kind of affection, but even though I know that the animals care much more about the hay and grain I offer them than about me, I am not entirely ill-pleased. It is hard not to be flattered by flatterers, however aware one is of their ulterior motives, and animals are the greatest flatterers in the world. To be greeted each morning by an ecstatic chorus, to hear them acknowledge my presence with delighted mooings and bleatings and bellowings, with honks and quacks and squeals and cackles, with a rush of anxious feet as I open the barn door, is to experience a sensation of indispensability that would try the humility of a saint.

And after all, the animals are right: I am vitally important to them. If I did not feed them, they would starve. Our attachment to one another is satisfyingly direct in comparison with the shifting nuances of human relationships so emphasized by the Christmas season. Feeding a dozen barnyard animals is one gift-giving activity to which there are absolutely no strings attached except for the baling twine. I count that a blessing.

There are other unexpected blessings to be had at this time of year. We come upon them with surprised appreciation as our perspective changes, now that the season has truly enveloped us. The snow itself, which loomed as a threat for so long before it actually made its appearance, now reveals itself in the character of a gift.

The children are the first to recognize this and to delight in it. With happy abandon, they plunge into the new element as if it were a summer ocean. They make snow forts, snow angels, snow men, and snow women of every imaginable size and variety. We adults take a little longer to adjust. We wait for a clear day, strap on snowshoes or skis, and find that parts of the landscape that were all but denied us during hunting season and throughout the rains of late fall are once again accessible.

As in a dream, we pass unaccompanied through pastures that are alive with curious holsteins during the summer. We glide unseen across our neighbor's empty hayfields and the sugar woods where he will be tapping trees in March. We move unimpeded, thanks to the smooth uniformity of the snow now covering it, over an unused field grown so thick with ground hemlock that you could not negotiate it comfortably at any other time of year. The land is ours again.

Indoors, we discover the gift of centering, of drawing into our own family core. The snowdrifts close in around us, night falls earlier, and the family necessarily spends more time together—usually in the kitchen, the coziest room in the house. We read more stories aloud, play more games, bake Christmas cookies, make popcorn, and work on holiday projects. By the end of February we may be at each other's throats in a frenzy of communal cabin fever, but in December, still early in the season, we are content to be caught up in the festivity of togetherness.

The great gift, of course, is the gift of Christmas itself. In our town, we have caroling on Christmas Eve, and a candlelight service is held in the Congregational Church, built over a century ago in the most poignantly picturesque Christmas setting I have ever seen. Not many places in America have the nineteenth-century–greeting-card look of the northern New England hill towns in December, with their white clapboard houses and white church spires, and not too many communities carry on the old traditions the way these communities do.

On the last Sunday morning before the holiday, people of all ages gather at the church to pack baskets and boxes with homebaked goods and small remembrances. The smaller children decorate a forest of tiny evergreens with popcorn balls, colored yarn, and a multitude of other ornaments they have made. Then, by ones and twos, alone or with parents and friends, the children travel the roads with the baskets, the boxes, and the trees.

They stop only at certain houses, only leave their gifts with certain people, although it is not a matter of calculated charity. This is a simpler offering, directed at those people who might need an extra bit of Christmas this year: the old; the sick; people who live alone; people who have had a recent sorrow; people who, because of infirmity or illness, may not be able to leave their homes to take part in any of the holiday celebrations. Like the deer in our woods, they are confined by circumstance to one small corner of existence, and they welcome the children the way the children welcome Christmas morning.

If only one could do as well by the citizens of the woods and pastures, all the creatures who are unaffected by my passing as I travel the old logging roads on my skis. I can tell that they have been here before me: two fat-pawed back footprints of a snowshoe hare overtake the delicate smaller prints of the front feet in a repetitive pattern across my trail, while the long, light line of doglike paw marks from a red fox traverses our meadow. When I turn the corner of the trail that leads to the brook, I can see the tiny traces left by a mouse's feet and tail as it explored the roots of a large tamarack. This mouse track ends neatly and safely near a little hole in the snow. I have seen other, similar tracks, abruptly arrested amid signs of a much greater commotion: a scuffed indentation in the path, the barely visible sweep of large wings across the snow. Owls, and sometimes hawks, are still abroad on December nights, and they, too, are hungry.

Often there is a thaw around Christmastime, and the brook runs freely for a while. Then I will see many more tracks: deep cloven prints left by deer, light tracks that might belong to a fisher our dog treed in this area in the fall, and once a puzzling trough-like trail lined with small prints very close together, which our woods-wise neighbor identified as the characteristic winter track of the porcupine, with its low body and small feet. But even if there is no thaw, the few animal tracks that are visible will all lead to one small hole where the brook runs fastest and deepest, a place the ice never completely covers up.

At this very spot, I lost a tin cup to a Christmas impulse. I used to carry the cup when I went cross-country skiing, in order to drink at the brook. One holiday afternoon, I hung it on a broken spruce branch that reaches out over the water, just in case anyone else should need it. Probably it was a futile gesture. But I figured that you never can tell who might be passing through this part of the world at this time of year, thirsty enough to appreciate a cup full of good will.

WOOD AND BLOOD

In the winter, dinner party conversation among the new settlers in Vermont is generally confined to two topics: wood and blood. This is how it happens: Back-to-the-Country couples get together with friends for an evening, gather around the wood stove for a drink before dinner, and find that the first topic of common interest is staring them in the face. As we warm ourselves inside and out, we begin to talk about stoves.

This tends to be a lengthy and detailed discussion with a number of distinct phases, beginning with a comparison of the merits of Vermont Castings, Jotul, Shenandoah, Sam Daniels, and the like, and moving on to a period of anxious worrying about such things as creosote buildup, chimney fires, and the toxic potential of certain fumes emitted during the burning of wood. We share our experience of harvesting trees for firewood or contemplate the advantages of faster-burning as opposed to slower-burning species. Before we've exhausted our subject entirely, we're almost sure to cover the whole range of wood stove accessories on the market, from temperature gauges to copper kettles to mitten racks.

From wood, we move invariably to slaughter. It's an easy conversational step from burning one's own wood to growing one's own meat, whether it be beef, poultry, lamb, or pork, and of course the most challenging thing about growing one's own meat is butchering the animals. So that's the way the talk goes: wood and blood, every time.

I prefer blood myself. It isn't as gory as it sounds, and it offers a variety of lessons to be learned. Our "rubber goose" is a good example. The trouble began when we sent a friend out into the barnyard to catch a goose. We neglected to warn him that we had been raising geese for twelve years, and anything he could catch easily was probably so old and tough that it wouldn't be worth eating. Later, my indignant family sat around the table while a very polite guest, a logger, remarked, "Well, it's all right if you kind of chew across the grain."

Then there was the sad experience of a friend's two children, who became vegetarians at an early age after living through the raising and then butchering of a most personable family pig. Those of us who rear children in the country do so with the expectation that they will learn important things here, and they do. It is also true that we as parents can rarely predict or control the nature of this education, no matter how much we try.

I must say, though, that the people whose company I really enjoy at these evening gatherings are the lapsed vegetarians or, to describe them more accurately, the born-again carnivores. Like other converts, these people have an all-embracing attitude. They eat everything. They eat all those parts of the animal that you and I tell the butcher he can keep. Not long ago I attended a luncheon meeting of a local women's group, and the hostess surprised some of us by serving tongue. We are a sort of soup-and-cheese-and-homemade-bread crowd, but I, for one, thought the tongue was delicious—much better than the last time I had tasted it, under threat of finishing it or going to bed without dessert. The only jarring note came when our hostess passed the platter around to our rather chatty group and said, without blinking an eye, "My husband thought this was the most appropriate thing to cook for you ladies."

Of course, her husband was not dining with us at the time. He was off somewhere "working with wood," as country husbands so often are. If you think you detect a bitter note here, you are right. I know I speak for many wives when I say that wood has severely tried my patience in recent years, and frankly, I'm sick of it.

For those of you who may be unfamiliar with this phrase, I am not thinking of the craft of woodworking when I say "working with wood." Nor am I referring to the occupation known in this part of the world as "working in the woods," which I have heard covers everything from logging to grand larceny. I am talking about the work engaged in by any household that depends upon wood for its winter warmth. The undertaking may include the whole family—husband, wife, and children—but more often than not the husband does by far the greatest share. This is one family enterprise for which the traditional division of labor still holds. Perhaps it appeals to some men for that very reason, although many will reject such a notion. Still, I can remember my jealous rage as I watched my husband walk off to cut wood one afternoon many years ago. I was standing by the window, folding laundry and wondering what to cook for supper, while two small and very fussy daughters circled me like mosquitoes about to draw blood. Off at the edge of the field was Richard, in plain view, strolling toward the woods with the dog by his side. I was just as furious at the two of them, loping along in their freedom, as I was with the toddlers at my knees.

Years later, my perspective has changed. I am no longer angry with my daughters, who are less fussy these days, or with my husband, who has since suffered one of the dozen serious wood-related accidents we have heard about in our area over the last decade. No, it's the wood itself I can't stand.

Not trees. I have nothing against trees so long as they stay rooted. I love maples and beeches and white pines and even those disheveled-looking dead elms that stand gauntly in the dooryards of old farms, serving as both memorial and warning.

My grudge is against lumber and firewood, logs and stumpage and board feet, cords and stacks and piles. Nor do I think much of chain saws. But I don't like axes any better, and as for pulp hooks and peaveys, and that miracle of modern engineering, the log-splitter—well, you just don't want to hear about it.

Aside from the risks, the work itself is devastating. Unless you have absolutely nothing else to do with those hours, nothing that can bring in money to pay for fuel—even wood!—how can it possibly be economical to heat your home in such a time-consuming way? I can remember Richard spending countless days of his life in the process: cutting wood, splitting it, lifting it and loading it on the wagon behind the tractor, then bringing it home and unloading it through the bulkhead into the basement, then stacking it. And all through the winter he was unstacking it again, to load into the furnace day and night, piece by back-breaking piece.

I never understood just why he got so much satisfaction from these labors, but perhaps that was because I was not involved. Oh, I carried wood and loaded the stove, and still do, but the lengths he cut for the furnace were too heavy for me. He was afraid that if I tried to load those, I would get a log stuck halfway in and halfway out of the furnace door some February night and burn the house down.

I'll admit there were times when I was tempted to such an extreme, especially after he was injured, but I never voiced my feelings. It would not have been tactful or compassionate. Instead, I drove my husband to the hospital in silence, merely gritting my teeth when he looked through the window at a row of young trees he had set out the previous year and observed between spasms of pain, "Those birches are coming along nicely, I see." I sat quietly in the X-ray waiting room, listened patiently to the orthopedic surgeon, and waited in the hospital with much anxiety but with some composure while his spine was being fused. I will confess, however, to a great surge of relief when I heard the first words my husband uttered as he came out from under the anesthetic seven hours later. He looked at me, blinked, tried to swallow, and said very clearly, "Goddamn wood!"

It sounded as if he were going to renounce the stuff forever. There certainly was a span of time when all the signs pointed in that direction. We began to use the oil furnace, which had sat idle the whole previous winter, and during his recovery from surgery Richard occupied himself with calculations of relative costs. He came up with the discovery that our medical bills, over and above what was paid by our insurance, were higher than our oil costs had ever been.

"I must have been crazy!" he marveled. What could I say?

My hopes were further bolstered by an evening spent with some Back-to-the-Country backsliders, hosted by a wonderful couple who had sold everything from their goats to the Garden Way cart in order to finance a business in town. Gleefully, and with growing self-mockery, we all acknowledged our masochistic follies of the past, like outdoor plumbing and wood stoves, and divulged our sinful comforts of the present, like thermostats and trips to Florida.

It was a delightful party, full of silly stories and ripe with the promise of self-indulgences that New Englanders rarely permit themselves. I still remember it with pleasure and with a touch of wistfulness, because naturally the mood didn't last. We may not be the rural purists that we were ten years ago, but in fact, most of the people at that party are still heating their homes with wood.

It's a hard habit to break, and the smell of woodsmoke is one of the most insidious things I know. It is easy to become addicted to it and to the feeling of comfort you get when the whole family is gathered around the wood stove at the end of the day. The dog and cat stretch out on the old rug, the children curl up with their books, and my husband comes in with an armload of logs that leave little pieces of bark all over his sweater and the floor.

"Real men," he announces to forestall my disapproval, "don't use wood carriers." I shrug, although I don't see how our wood carrier, a plain canvas affair with leather handles, could possibly compromise his masculinity. Mostly I am grateful that he is carrying small, stove-sized logs rather than the mammoths that used to go into the wood furnace we no longer have. I am aware as I watch him that we haven't kicked the wood habit entirely, but at least it is more under control. "Yes, we do wood," I think to myself excusingly, "but only in moderation."

I don't believe there is any other way to go, given our circumstances and the nature of the winters here in Vermont. The alternatives are unsatisfactory at best, and sometimes downright unsettling. I met a poor soul the other day, a longtime refugee from midtown Manhattan, wandering around in the middle of winter with a strange, glazed look in his eyes. He greeted me cheerfully enough, but then he began to reveal his real feelings. He said he had given up all thought of ever leaving Vermont in the winter. "When I lived in New York," he said, "I used to go to Hawaii all the time. Florida, the Caribbean. . . . But I've lived right here for fourteen years now, and do you know what? I don't *want* to be warm anymore!"

S · P · R · I · N · G

LAMBING AND SUGARING

"If it weren't for lambing and sugaring, I'd never make it through this time of year."

Someone said this to me once, in the drizzle and gloom of early March, and I couldn't agree with her more. At this season, below-zero temperatures and bleak winds alternate with slushy thaws for so long that if you didn't have the sheep and the syrup, you'd go crazy.

The sheep are the first to save us from our spring–creeping dementia. Lambing is an annual godsend for the bored, the cabin-fevered, and those who simply enjoy being bossy. I have always found it extremely satisfying to throw my weight around among sheep, and not terribly difficult. For instance, when I went to a neighbor's barn not long ago to check on her new lambs and their mothers, I had no qualms about following the instructions she had left pinned to the barn door: "Throw ewes down and hook babies on to suck, unless you're not dressed for it."

It was a courteous afterthought, but I'm always dressed for it, more or less, so I went right to work. One after the other, I grabbed two ewes by their legs and tumbled them over onto their sides, then coaxed two young lambs to nurse. The ewes were docile, the lambs were hungry, and I left the barn with an intoxicating sense of power and beneficence that lasted all the rest of that day.

Aside from megalomania, the sheep and their lambs also give me a wonderful feeling of peace and well-being and the promise of better days ahead. I love being inside a barn with a group of ewes and new lambs. I love the warmth, the hay and animal smells, and above all the noises: the mothers and babies calling to each other, the rustlings and creakings as they move about the sheep room, and often the drumming sound of rain on the roof, telling me that winter's grip is weakening. At these times the barn with its newborn creatures feels like a kind of Noah's Ark, carrying a cargo of resurrection safely through the rough weather and darkness of early spring.

But then again, Noah had only two sheep. I don't suppose they gave him much trouble. Our own experience has been widely varied, and over the years it has taught us our basic lambing philosophy, which goes something like this: When you raise sheep you must accept the fact that some lambs will survive the worst possible birthing conditions whereas others, as a friend sourly put it, "are born trying to die." To those you may devote your best efforts and give every type of assistance available—shots of glucose in saline, supplementary feedings day and night, even force-feedings through stomach tubes as a last resort—but it makes no difference. They simply refuse to live.

Those who do survive, usually a majority even in an inexperienced sheep owner's worst year, bring not only the pleasures and occasional profits of success, but also the joy of watching the lambs themselves. They race and jump and butt each other and leap on top of their resting mothers' backs and then leap off again and race some more, delighted with one another and with their own momentum. Even if the snow lies deep on the ground all around them, the lambs are convinced, and convince the rest of us, that spring is in the air.

For many sheep owners, the atmosphere of the new season is also maple-scented. And with any luck, by the time sugaring begins in earnest with the strong sap runs of late March and early April, the most difficult lambing time is over. The newborns are now sturdy and frisking, with little need of human supervision, and the shepherds are free to turn their attention to taps and buckets and boiling equipment, to the apparatus and alchemy of evaporation.

"I'll probably always do it, just because I enjoy it," a friend confided as he drove a tractor through mud and slush and mealy spring snow, up into the heart of a sloping sugar orchard. Near the top of the hill the sugarhouse was spewing steam in all directions, like a teakettle that has been too long on the boil. From a distance these buildings look active, agitated, poised for takeoff. Inside, they are dark and moist and sweetly infernal with the red-hot glow of the firebox as it is stoked with wood over and over to keep the temperature constant in the pans, and the fragrant mists that rise and billow and obscure the view like thick fog, then disappear entirely only to rise again within seconds, engulfing human figures wherever they stand.

There is a touch of magic and mystery in both barn and sugarhouse in early spring, and a bit of the midwife in shepherd and sugarmaker alike, as each tends to the biology of the new season. My own children watch over our half-dozen sheep and our four sap buckets as if they think spring itself may be born in one of our lambing pens or distilled in that steaming kettle over the kitchen stove. I know better, of course. I've lived in Vermont long enough to know that spring would come eventually even without the lambs and the syrup. But I've also lived here long enough to know that it just wouldn't be the same.

POULTRY WARS

I recently read, in one of those magazines that present human problems in numerical order, that the prime cause of conflict between married couples these days is Money. I was not surprised. Nor was I startled to learn that Children come next (children are invariably close to the action, whatever it is), and that further down the list are such perennial favorites as Sex and In-laws, followed by a few more troublemakers like Education and Life-style. What did surprise me was that nowhere in this collection did I see the word *Poultry.* During all our years of country living my husband and I have experienced so much bitter conflict over the care and protection of barnyard birds that I was disappointed to find we stood unrepresented by the list makers.

I have my own list. In fact, I have all our poultry fights titled in my mind, much the way historians label individual battles in major wars. I recall the Man of Action Affair a decade ago, which centered on a family of barnyard ducks (technically waterfowl, and hence not the subject of a poultry fight at all). Several years later came the Frozen Silkie Encounter, a lively skirmish involving a dozen Japanese Silkie bantams and a spell of subzero February weather. Last on the list are the Peacock Wars, which stretch out over five years and are characterized by two distinct passages of arms. The first was the Wild Peacock Fracas. It was dramatic and colorful, but short-lived. The second was the Wet Peacock Engagement, which began about a year ago and remains unresolved at this writing.

The first pair of ducks, the ones that started all the trouble, looked harmless enough. Soon after they arrived on our barnyard, they brought forth a dozen black-and-brown ducklings. Our whole family delighted in watching the duck family splash in barnyard puddles and walk single file to drink and dabble at the overflow from our spring-fed trough.

Not long after that, however, the ducks began to disappear. One morning, two ducklings were missing at the trough. The next day, two others as well as the mother were gone, and a trail of feathers led under the fence into the tall grass. The children and I rounded up as many of the remaining ducklings as we could and put them in the chicken room in the barn.

When Richard came home that evening, we begged him to do something. He was remarkably unenthusiastic. In my outrage, I spoke more hastily than I should have.

"My father was a man of action," I said bitterly, in front of the children. It was not a polite thing to say. Nonetheless, it brought results.

My husband took a mattress out to the barn that night. Before you draw the wrong conclusion, let me tell you that he also took a Winchester .32 caliber Special and a twelve-volt flashlight. Next he took a duck from the chicken room and placed it in a closed wire cage in the middle of the barnyard. Then he went back into the barn to wait, under an open window.

He was there for several hours. It got darker and darker. Richard began to grow accustomed to the night noises around him: the peepers in the swamp, the call of an owl in the pine woods, the muffled rattle of a truck far off on the main road. Then, suddenly, all the noises stopped. "It was like one of those Westerns we saw in the ninth grade," he told me later. Out of nowhere a dim shape arose and moved in the direction of the caged duck. Richard cocked the gun and readied his finger on the flashlight switch.

The trouble was, this was not a fox, skunk, or raccoon. It was an animal without stealth. It did not lurk, creep, or even sneak. Instead, it dodged and feinted rapidly this way and that, jabbering as if demented.

It was a fisher, moving at lightning speed among the grazing horses, cows, and sheep, while the alarmed duck began to quack wildly. My husband quickly turned on the flashlight, blinding himself in its glare. For the first few seconds he couldn't see anything at all. After that he could see only the duck, which had quieted down nicely, mesmerized in the flashlight's beam.

I don't think the peacocks were my idea, although appearances may be against me. It is true that I gave the original pair to my husband for a birthday present. He had been fascinated by peacocks for years and had dreams of seeing them stroll proudly about our barnyard, tails spread wide, lending our somewhat haphazard environment all the exquisite grace and fine coloring of a Persian miniature. Richard, a photographer and therefore a visual artist, has dreams like that all the time. I am a writer. Instead of exquisite dreams, I retain vague, often troubled, literary memories. Insofar as I can recall her essay, Flannery O'Connor, who raised peacocks in Georgia, made the birds seem interesting but not desirable and gave them a markedly southern stamp.

I was shocked, therefore, to open our local newspaper a week before my husband's birthday one year and see an advertisement for a going-out-of-business sale in which two young male peacocks were listed among the other merchandise. I rushed off to the sale and returned home with the two peacocks, a quantity of information about their care and habits, and some private misgivings.

My husband was delighted with his present. For a week he spent much time with the peacocks in the chicken room, watching their movement and feeding them. By the end of the week they were eating out of his hand, he boasted. It was time to let them out to strut.

I disagreed. I didn't trust the peacocks. They had shifty eyes, I said. Richard scoffed at me. These birds would never leave us, he claimed, because they knew where their food was. Between strutting sessions they would return for meals, and at night they would roost, as peacocks are known to do, on the highest point in the area—in this case, the roof of the barn. After a bitter altercation, I yielded. They were his peacocks, after all.

A preoccupation with Persian miniatures must have clouded my husband's mind. The highest point in the area is the top of East Hill, just across the valley from our farm. We could hear the peacocks calling to each other late the next afternoon as they soared off toward it, on powerful wings whose existence we had all but forgotten in our discussions of strutting and strolling. We don't know where they flew after that.

The next four peacocks came from Virginia, several years later. These birds were a good deal smaller than the others. At first they were unprepossessing in color and tended to huddle together in one corner of the chicken room and blink. They lived there with the chickens all through the cold winter, becoming larger and most attractive as the spring advanced, with blue heads and multicolored feathers now apparent.

I knew that it would not be long before my husband's thoughts turned to strutting and strolling and so forth, but I was ready for him.

"Peacocks," I said, "are not smart about getting wet." I went on to tell him all the things I had learned along this line in the course of the years. (I got my information from another peacock owner.) Peacocks, like heroines in nineteenth-century novels, will take a chill from heavy dew or catch pneumonia after a slight shower, then go into a decline and expire.

My husband listened in disbelief for a while. Then he said to me, "You're trying to tell me that a breed of birds has survived through centuries without getting wet?"

"Think of turkeys!" I said. "Turkeys have the same kind of trouble. Turkeys aren't supposed to get wet."

"Not supposed to get wet!" he exploded. "Look at Les [a friend in the village]. He has turkeys all over the place. What do you think he does when it rains? Gives them all little umbrellas?"

We went on in that vein for several weeks, until a tragedy occurred that made me reconsider. Actually there were two tragedies. We lost two of our four peacocks, a male and a female, within a week of each other. We presumed at the time that they had died of some disease carried by the chickens. (We now know that peacocks mate for life and frequently die in pairs—when one dies, for whatever reason, its mate dies soon afterward.) We had only two male peacocks left, and I agreed sadly that we might as well let one of them live outdoors. The presence of his companion in the chicken room might keep him from straying from the barnyard, and in any case he would escape the germ that had killed the other two. If he wanted to strut a little while he was outside, that was his business. (This time we did not even consider letting both peacocks out together.)

Remembering our first experience, my husband clipped one wing of the liberated peacock, "just in case," although I protested. It seemed to me that a peacock that could not fly would stand less than a fighting (or roosting) chance against its predators. I needn't have worried. Those who strut can also streak. Once outside, our peacock, chased by a male guinea fowl with delusions of grandeur, took to the woods in record time and was last seen, by two young girls on bicycles, disappearing into the cedar swamp below our house.

The next morning, my neighbors down the road awoke to what they reported as "unearthly cries" under their window. A day later, the neighbor up the road called to ask if one of our peacocks was missing—his dog had chased one into the woods. On the third day, having made a three-mile circuit of the neighborhood, the peacock arrived back at our farm. He strutted around the driveway in an offhand manner for an hour or two, just to show us that he was able if he felt so inclined, and then went to stand patiently by the door of the chicken room, like a cat waiting to be let in. By this time, his friend on the inside was crying great joyful cries of welcome. When I opened the door, the wandering peacock sauntered inside, where he lives to this day.

I should assure you that it is possible to have some moments of peace and contentment with birds. One of our fondest recent memories concerns a day last fall when we dressed off a dozen chickens.

It was a beautiful late-October day, with cirrus clouds high overhead and a chill in the air. The sun shone in a golden way on the now-crisp maple leaves scattered about the yard and barn, and hot water steamed merrily in the twenty-gallon canner we had placed on an old door set on sawhorses in the barnyard. In the beginning, Richard did the part I couldn't stand doing, and later on I took care of the part he couldn't stand doing. But most of the time we just plucked together happily and enjoyed the day. We still look back on it with nostalgia, as The Day You and I Slaughtered the Chickens.

It's amazing what living in the country will do for a marriage, isn't it?

SPRING

Spring in Vermont is contrary, equivocal, the adolescent of the seasons. From late February to early May, we suffer its growing pains, gathering hope from the dripping of icicles and a few glimpses of bare ground, only to be thrown by an unexpected blizzard into a regressive midwinter's gloom. Spring here is like a seventh-grade boy whose voice is changing, or a thirteen-year-old girl in that awkward, back-and-forth period of life when one's interest hovers maddeningly between pierced ears and paper dolls. Each year, like the mother of a vacillating teenager, I am exasperated by a season that takes forever to grow up.

Farther south, where the year follows a milder climatic schedule, crocus tips appear beneath melting snowbanks in March, forsythia blooms in April, and robins fly in on the first warm wind. Here, we have nothing so predictable. Those months stage melodramatic contests between frost and thaw, and they end with a deluge of mud. We have muddy, impassable roads with muddy rivers running beside them, muddy driveways and muddy barnyards, muddy dogs and muddy children. All the dirt in the state seems to liquefy and find its way into kitchens and back hallways and braided rugs and wet wool mittens.

Then, just when it seems that we will be stuck forever with washed-out roads and bad weather, everything happens at once. No longer rebellious and indecisive, the season puts all of its energy into reaching full maturity. Anyone who looked in vain only days ago for "signs of spring" is hard put to keep track of them now. Coltsfoot blooms hardily along roadsides that showed dark, wet grit and last year's matted grass just moments before. Cowslip thrives ankle-deep in the marshy ground above the pasture, where the cows themselves will come to drink from the brook before the month is out. Red trillium, trout lily, and starflower appear everywhere underfoot as we walk up the abandoned road through the woods behind our house. The first spring peepers start up again in the swamp, and the wood thrush sings his brief, clear song at dusk. We feel the impossible softness of some furred or feathered barnyard infant and the benediction of spring sunshine touching the back of the neck as we kneel for the first time in the garden and smell moist earth that has just been turned up by the plow.

Memorial Day marks the last moment before we turn the corner into another season. In the town where I live, all of the citizens gather at the church on that day for a luncheon of homecooked hot dishes, rolls, salads, and pies. American flags and lilacs together decorate the tables, and after lunch everyone marches up to the graveyard on the hill, trailing along behind the veterans and the high-school band and the Girl Scouts. Speeches are made near the war memorial, on a patch of green grass. Young children carry the flags and the flowers from the lunch tables and place them near the graves of men who fell in conflicts dating from the Civil War to Vietnam.

Here is a sense of the great and small movements of time, of world history as it has touched the smaller communities of the earth, of the turning of the season and of life's seasons. The children's voices echo among the soldier's stones, the heady scent of lilac is everywhere. Soon it will be full-blown summer—perhaps tomorrow. Our brief north-country spring is over, and like the mother of that difficult child-adult who has grown up and left home at last, I think back over all the turmoil and the tenderness of the past season, and wonder where the time has gone.

S·U·M·M·E·R

SUMMER WORK

A country summer lives longest in the imagination, a midwinter night's dream of swimming holes and dusty roads and the deep, sweet odor of syringa filling an open window in July. We anticipate this season's coming for so long that when it finally arrives we almost can't believe it and definitely don't trust it not to slip away.

There is a tendency to approach our summers with a vanguard of activity that is frantic, feverish, and often premature. We plant our gardens too soon in defiance of the inevitable late frost, pump up the bicycle tires and sort out the summer shorts when the children have barely put away their muddy boots or even their mittens, and plan renovations on the house and barn before we've removed the insulation from around the foundations. We almost always rush this season, as if we need to get ahead of it before it seduces us into indolence with warm weather and our own winter dreams.

It is usually work, of course, that knits one season into the next in the country, and forces us to keep our heads and shore up the puritan ethic. We in New England are also workers by virtue of our nature and our climate. We have for generations been frugal, busy, and hard pressed by hard seasons. Nobody north of the Mason-Dixon line spends much time sipping mint juleps on a veranda. (I don't suppose many southerners do either, but I have always loved the luxurious, alien image of them that presents itself to my northern mind.) No matter how voluptuous the weather, we are much more apt to be making mint jelly from that wonderful patch of mint that grows by the brook in the pasture, or tearing up the porch because the floorboards finally did rot through this past winter so that anyone who steps onto our veranda risks his neck.

People who come to visit Vermont sometimes complain about the intensity of summer labors here, because these make life so inconvenient for them. The roads are always under construction, they say. Their friends are always haying or gardening or building something. Everybody is busy. Nobody has time for *fun*.

We respond immediately, indignantly. What do you think this is for us, vacation? This is the time of year when everything gets done around here: houses painted, food grown, frost heaves smoothed out and potholes filled in. (I am especially sensitive to this last point because I spent most of one summer on the West Side Drive in New York City where, it seems to me, the roads are never under construction no matter how much they need it. I almost left a rear axle under the George Washington Bridge.) We don't have time for fun, we scold our guests.

Some of us will add, if we're honest, that as a matter of fact, this *is* fun. Our kind of fun. This work is one of the reasons those of us who moved here from other parts of the country did so. This is why those of us who were born here stayed on. We may complain about it, sweat from it and over it, even wear ourselves out to the point where neighbor solicitously says to neighbor at the end of August, "You look tired, dear. Now for heaven's sake, don't overdo!" But the truth is that the things we do, and overdo, in order to make a living in the country or in order to keep our families and our homes going all year are also the things that make life worth living.

It isn't that we don't appreciate the beauty of the landscape, or that we don't know how to relax. It is that we relax best by living fully, and we appreciate the country most by participating wholeheartedly in the work that it has demanded and fostered for more than two centuries, work that involves family and home and community as well as the natural world with which we come in such direct contact season after season. This is why we are here.

THE FAT OF THE FALLOW

I did not have a vegetable garden last summer. It was my first garden-less summer in the seven years that constitute my family's life so far in northern Vermont. This was an odd sabbatical for me and not originally one of my choosing; it came about because our house, which has spent considerably more time than we have in this climate, was undergoing extensive repairs and renovations. I learned early in the spring that the process would require cement trucks, backhoes, bulldozers, and two dozen or more pairs of feet trampling my former gardening territory during the course of the summer. I heard with dismay that it would be impossible to use the spot I had worked over, weeded, and mulched for years, and had prepared so carefully the previous fall with wood ashes and well-aged chicken manure. At first, I entertained the idea of battling the field grass and the woodchucks for another piece of tillable soil, safe from the turmoil of construction but not in the path of the tractor and the mower blade at haying time.

The mere thought of starting another garden was depressing, and I was worn out just in anticipation of the work ahead. And then, as so often happens when one is weary, temptation struck. Why not give it up for a year? All of it—the seed catalogs, the decisions: escarole or romaine or 'Black-Seeded Simpson'? Row beans or pole? Do we really want to plant Swiss chard again this year, or do we all secretly prefer spinach? Do we have the moral fiber and inner strength to limit ourselves to a reasonable number of tomato plants, or will we have tomatoes blushing on every windowsill come Labor Day and the kitchen smelling of green tomato relish until Thanksgiving? What about squash? Can we face another onslaught of zucchini and its relatives—more numerous and demanding in August than my own?

"Well, frankly, I'm sick and tired of being bullied all summer by a bunch of vegetables," my husband grumbled as mutiny spread throughout the family. We decided that we were through with the radishes, and the carrots as well, with seeds and shoots so tiny that planting and thinning them practically required a microscope. We were fed up with planting enough corn to feed our family and the raccoons, too; tired of fighting the frost for the tomatoes, and the cutworms for the cabbages and cauliflowers. As for the peas, they are the worst of all. From the moment in mid-May when the first smug, early planter asks us quietly, "Got your peas in yet?" to the time in late September when we pull up the posts and pea fences and wearily roll up the wire to store in the barn, they plague us with confusion and contrariness. There is currently a new T-shirt being sold in our area. It depicts a succulent, split-pea pod full of tender, green fruit and is inscribed with the slogan—a pun recycled from the antiwar movement of the 1960s—Give Peas a Chance. It seems to me that somebody should invent a rebuttal garment (a hair shirt, perhaps) allowing gardeners equal time. Peas have never given us a chance. They are the peskiest, most ornery vegetables I know. If you plant them too early, they sprout immediately and freeze, and if you don't plant them early enough, they languish in the hot weather. When you are about a week away from harvesting the whole crop for table or freezer, having tested individual pea pods twice a day to judge their readiness, you visit your sister and come back to find that overnight the peas have gone from unripe to overripe. Peas could drive a person to drink.

A few swift financial calculations also convinced my husband and me that we would be doing ourselves a favor by giving up the garden. We would save time and earn money, because the time previously devoted to gardening would now go to my writing and my husband's photography. Hours once spent in planting and weeding, in harvesting and freezing or canning, would be spent at the desk and in the darkroom. From now on, instead of growing our vegetables, we would earn them. We would cultivate our imaginations instead of the soil and reap innumerable benefits.

We learned a lot last summer about gardening and about ourselves. One of the happiest things we learned is that not having a garden in a gardening community amounts to a public service. Everybody plants too much; everybody eventually gets tired of picking and shelling and freezing peas, of snapping beans, of boiling beets, and even of husking corn. On the other hand, nobody raised in New England can stand to see good food go to waste. Therefore, we enjoyed unlimited freeloading rights last summer, and best of all, we didn't solicit fresh vegetables; we were showered with them. Only a three-month-old kitten is harder to give away than zucchini in August.

The first blow to our self-satisfied abstinence came when we learned that we do not like iceberg lettuce. In maligning all vegetables earlier in the spring, we had forgotten about garden lettuce. It is my favorite vegetable, and as far as I can tell, everybody else's, too. People do not readily dole out their home-grown lettuce, and why should they? It is delicious and easy to plant and tend. When it needs thinning, the very thinnings are delicious, too. Why, oh why, I wondered in midsummer over yet another meal of supermarket iceberg, didn't I plant at least a little bit of garden lettuce?

The next blow was dealt by a bag of green beans. Good old trustworthy, never-fail green beans. One afternoon a tired neighbor handed me a grocery bag full of them, crisp and unsnapped. I opened the bag and was overwhelmed by the familiar smell of warm earth, fresh-picked legumes, and brown paper. I almost wept with nostalgia, not to mention guilt. What harm had green beans ever done to me that I should abandon them? Not once during all the years of planting have they failed to repay every bit of my effort a hundredfold—sometimes even a thousandfold—which is their only fault. They simply flourish in their orderly fashion, year after year, and nothing fazes them. Even after a flood one summer, when a family of barnyard ducks swam about the garden for several days, diving down occasionally to nibble at submerged pea pods, the beans survived. Beans had given me seven years of faithful service, and I had rejected them without a thought.

"These carrots are yucky. Even the rabbit won't eat them." Suddenly both my children were clamoring for carrots wrapped in dirt rather than plastic. They longed to run out "like last year" to pull up the fat little fingerlings of new carrots from the summer soil.

One after another, the ghosts of homegrown vegetables came flitting back into our minds: huge, fat cabbages that crunch into wavy, segmented halves with one solid thwack of the kitchen knife; shiny green peppers; tiny, crisp cucumbers; the first bite of a buttered ear of sweet corn, steaming hot and only five minutes off the stalk. We remembered when our youngest daughter picked a ripe tomato and ate it as if it were an apple, the red skin softly splitting under her little white teeth, a trickle of the warm, sweet juice escaping from a corner of her mouth, the delight on her face.

The fact is, homegrown vegetables taste better than anything else on earth. I hate to admit it, but it's true. One's very own vegetables, like one's own children, have a beauty unsurpassed by anyone else's. My children loved their first, fist-sized, homegrown Halloween pumpkin better than all the roadside giants we had bought before or have since. After a summer of sampling many delicious varieties, I still prefer my own corn and my own string beans. I don't know whether it's due to their relative freshness—the period between garden and table can be wonderfully short when you cook your own vegetables—or whether I have a fondly biased memory. The vegetables of memory and dreams are, I suspect, even tastier than the ones we actually harvest and have a life and influence all their own.

If we ever have a garden again, it will have to be a much smaller garden, something practical and suited to our needs. There will be lettuce in it, and beans, and a few carrots for the children if they insist. And definitely a pumpkin or two for Halloween. Then there's corn; you can't really have a garden without corn. We'll have at least one tomato plant—well, two, just in case something happens to the first one, which is likely in this climate. And in a way, it will make sense to plant a few peas again, because those old posts and the chicken wire are perfectly good. We won't forget cucumbers or peppers, either. But if we were to grow cucumbers and pumpkins, we might as well have some squash in the same area, for convenience. They can all be planted in hills and mingled together: cucumbers, pumpkins, zucchini—zucchini? Oh, why not. But I won't plant any radishes at all next time. You have to draw the line somewhere.

WALKS

In the country there is always a reason for a walk. We seem to *need* a reason, as if the bare experience were not enough in itself. We walk to get somewhere (to school, to work), or to get something (exercise, the mail), or to add to our knowledge (bird walks, mushroom walks, wildflower walks sponsored by our local nature museums) or to our larders (nut and berry walks, walks to the orchard in the fall). A walk may mark a rhythm for the day: the skipping excitement of a schoolchild heading down a gravel road to the bus stop early in the morning, or the slow, swinging amble of cows coming home to be milked at dusk. I know many people who walk because of their occupations or to comply with a planned health-and-recreation schedule. I also know a few who walk for sorrow and one or two who walk for joy.

A French friend once compared the refreshment of walking to that of taking a bath, using the phrase *"bain de foule, bain de forêt"* to explain that there were two kinds of bathers in this case: those who bathed in crowds and those who bathed in the forest. It is true that walking through a busy village in the late afternoon is very different from striking out into the woods, but it is also true that the observations and encounters of village walking are just as pleasurable as those of a more sylvan nature. I like to watch the passage of light into shadow on the individual houses toward evening, and the movements of friends up and down the street—someone is taking the dog out for a last walk, someone else is opening up the church for choir practice, a third person is taking laundry in from the porch clothesline at the end of the day. The ebb and flow of village life at any given moment is just as fascinating as most phenomena of the Vermont woods and meadows.

There are definite quantitative differences in walking styles. Some people only walk as far as the mailbox or the post office, and at certain seasons exhibit great pride at having been so venturesome, while others never do less than five miles a day, whatever the weather. There are also qualitative differences, and these can sometimes cause conflicts between individual walkers. My father used to complain that walking with my mother was like strolling with "a munching cow!" She did not stop to graze, of course, but to observe birds overhead through her binoculars, or to examine and identify interesting species of plants at her feet. My mother tends to be a small-focus, investigative, live-in-the-moment walker, while my father was a long-legged strider, wanting to exercise his muscles and really *get* somewhere.

I have noticed this difference often, though not always, between men and women who walk together. I have noticed, too, that when they walk separately, men and women both may walk to achieve a perspective, but usually it is a different perspective. When I first moved to the country I knew a number of young couples who were homesteading or renovating old homes here while at the same time raising new families. It was a wonderfully exhilarating time in our lives, despite the hard work our lives required, or perhaps because of it. I remember taking many energetic walks with my contemporaries, and observing even then that the men and the women walked with different objectives in mind. The women walked to get *away* from the household routines and from the house itself briefly, to drink in the fresh air and freedom of a larger view. The men, on the other hand, invariably set off walking toward some specific spot from which they could look *back* at the house they had been working on and at the fruits of their various labors there: the new chimney, the woodpile. Women tended to hunger for a taste of the infinite, while men preferred a view that included their own carefully tended piece of property.

This business of walking to look at a view—any view—has always been fascinating to me. I can't help wondering what it is that each of us yearns to have a view *of*. And anyway, isn't the square foot of grass and ground under our own feet, with all its rich animal and vegetable variety, just as significant a subject to study as the panorama of the White Mountains in the distance? Certainly some views are more spectacular than others, and there are towns where property tax is associated directly with the appraised value of one's view, but it is, as always, a question of what people choose to consider valuable. There are those who would hike twenty miles into a state forest to catch a glimpse of a pileated woodpecker but have little interest in the less exotic birds who gather in our own dooryards. Others will stop at half the houses in town during an afternoon of visiting, but are exhausted at the very thought of a walk in the woods.

Our walks reflect our lives and our characters, I think, wherever we decide to walk to and whatever we choose to look at on the way or when we get there. The view from the kingdom is ultimately and profoundly a view *of* the kingdom, and the prospect will depend, for each of us, on our deepest and truest vision of what that kingdom might be.

LIST OF PHOTOGRAPHS

ACKNOWLEDGMENTS

We would like to thank the people of the
Northeast Kingdom, the farmers, loggers, and
homesteading newcomers who let Richard
photograph them as they made a living from
this hard but beautiful land. Also, David
Lyman who encouraged Richard to put these
photographs into a book, and Dale Parker of
Boris Color Labs in Boston, who supervised
the initial lab work. Special acknowledgment
to Nancy Price Graff for her inspiration,
editorial labors, and the title of this book.